PRACTICAL LIVING FOR THE CHILD

Rev. Dianne Langlois Dorsey

authorHOUSE®

AuthorHouse™
1663 Liberty Drive
Bloomington, IN 47403
www.authorhouse.com
Phone: 1 (800) 839-8640

Published by AuthorHouse 08/19/2016

ISBN: 978-1-5246-2450-7 (sc)
ISBN: 978-1-5246-2449-1 (e)

Print information available on the last page.

Any people depicted in stock imagery provided by Thinkstock are models,
and such images are being used for illustrative purposes only.
Certain stock imagery © Thinkstock.

This book is printed on acid-free paper.

Because of the dynamic nature of the Internet, any web addresses or
links contained in this book may have changed since publication and
may no longer be valid. The views expressed in this work are solely those
of the author and do not necessarily reflect the views of the publisher,
and the publisher hereby disclaims any responsibility for them.

Scripture quotations marked KJV are from the Holy Bible, King James
Version (Authorized Version). First published in 1611. Quoted from the KJV
Classic Reference Bible, Copyright © 1983 by The Zondervan Corporation.

Lovingly Dedicated To

God and His Darling Son, Jesus
My Husband, Irvin
My daughter, Philana
My Grandson, Sherrod
My Grand-daughter, Greiana
My mother, Alberta
My mother-in-law, Victoria
My editor, Cindy Hurst
My family, friends, and co-workers
The children of the world

INTRODUCTION

This book is written for the parents who need God's helping hands in raising their children in His grace. It is also for the children who need to read and understand God's word of their lives.

When a Bible is not handy, use this as a quick reference for wisdom and strength and to do what is right in the sight of God. It is for children to better understand the role their parents play. It is also a useful book for children who seemingly refuse to do what is right; to help them set goals and to understand when things go wrong. It is to assist them in understanding love, joy, sin, obeying parents, education, money, kindness, and turning to God in the hour of need.

This book was written for those children who feel alone, abused, frightened, with low self-esteem, and who feel unloved. Reading this offering will help you to surrender your all to God and teach you how to go to Him in prayer. It will teach repentance and why we repent.

Satan has been trying to destroy our children and we need to wage war over him and his demon spirits. We need to take our children back and allow God to guide them.

Included in this book are scripture references from the King James Version of the Holy Bible.

I finished this book in August 2006, just a few hours before Hurricane Katrina hit New Orleans, Louisiana. I lost everything—except these pages. When the water began to rise in my home, it stopped right at the top of my dresser, where the pages of this manuscript lied. They never got wet. Even though Satan tried to tell me this book is worthless, I was determined to have it published. Satan does not want anything good to go through to bless someone. By writing this book, I have stepped out on faith, believing it is meant to be.

This book will help some people. Others, it may not. You be the judge. It's here!

PRACTICAL LIVING
FOR THE CHILD

How do I begin? What do I say to the children of the world? Let me start by saying, the greatest love the world has ever read about, is the love of God. *"For God so loved the world that He gave His only begotten Son, that whosoever believed in Him should not perish, but have everlasting life."* **John 3:16** He did this so that we may live and be able to repent (ask God forgiveness of our sins) so we may be with God after we die.

There are so many types of love. But the love that God gives us is the ultimate! If we ask and believe Him, we can have this great love. I am not saying for you to put your life on the line for anyone; only to love one another as brothers and sisters in Christ. *"For love is strong as death; jealousy is cruel as the grave."* **Song of Solomon 8:6** *"God have loved thee with an everlasting love."* **Jeremiah 31:3** *"Love your enemies, bless them that curse you, do good to them that hate you and pray for them which despitefully use and persecute you."* **Matthew 5:44** *"The fruit of the spirit is love, joy, peace, longsuffering, gentleness, goodness, faith."* **Galatians 5:22** *"No man has seen*

God at any time. If we love one another God will dwell in us, and His love is perfected in us." **1 John 4:12** *"God is familiar with all my ways before a word is on my tongue, You know it completely."* **Psalm 139:4** *"Where can I flee from Your presence?"* **Psalm 139:7** What I am trying to do is show you the greatness of love! It is better to be loved and give love, in this life, than never to have loved at all.

You are probably asking, "How can I teach my children about the Bible when I am a sinner?" *"Therefore, just as by one man sin entered into the world, and death by sin; and so death passed upon all men, for that all have sinned—For until the law sin was in the world, but sin is not imputed when there is no law. Nevertheless, death reigned from Adam to Moses, even over them that had not sinned after the likeness of Adam's transgression, who is the figure of Him that was to come."* **Romans 5:12-14** Satan tempts us by the lust of the flesh, eyes, and pride of life. This is what he uses to trap us. When we are taught the Word as children, we have a better outlook on life and a stronger prayer life. In other words, we need to form a personal relationship with God.

The word of God states: "Train up a child in the way he should go; and when he is old, he will not depart from it." **Proverbs 22:6** What has happened to the basics that we know?

> *"Our Father, which art in heaven, Hallowed by Thy name. Thy kingdom come. Thy will be done in earth, as it is in heaven. Give us this day our daily bread. And forgive us our debts, as we forgive our debtors. And lead us*

> *not into temptation, but deliver us from evil.*
> *For Thine is the kingdom and the power and*
> *the glory forever. Amen."* **Matthew 6:9-13**

What about this one?

> *Now I lay me down to sleep; I pray the Lord*
> *my soul to keep.*
>
> *If I die before I wake, I pray the Lord my soul*
> *to take.*

When I was a child, my mama taught me those prayers. I said one prayer, every night. You know, prayer was not just for our mama's and grand-mama's time. But they are for all times! *"For your Father knoweth what things ye have need of, before ye ask Him."* **Matthew 6:8**

The child must learn, first of all, *how* to love. In order to show love, he has to be shown love. Many people don't believe during sex when the sperm and egg meet, a life is formed. Please tell me, for the love of God, how when this happens, it is *not* a life? Okay. So you may say it is not a *life*, not a *person*. But let me tell you, in my opinion, why this is wrong. To make my point, I will use myself as an example.

Before I was born, my mother and father conceived me and from there, my cells began to form and grow. Dead things do not grow. So, at this point, I am *alive*. As long as my cells multiply from hundreds to many thousands, I am alive. Dead things do not reproduce because they are *dead*. So here I am, living and growing inside my mother's womb. Days later, my arms appear. Oh, look! I have legs! Do dead things grow arms and legs? Although, I am not yet born, I am very much alive and I continue to grow inside my mother. Inside her, I know no other comfort. I know her voice and I can feel her heart beat. When she sings or speaks to me, I am comforted.

God has formed Baby out of love and His love is being manifested in making this precious child! God's blessing is upon this tiny soul. He breathed life in her lungs as nurses and doctors, brings forth this bundle of joy. Yes, the child is born in this troubled world filled with shame and sin.

Parents/Children

Sin came into the world through the fall of Adam and Eve. Adam was created in the image of God. God gave Adam a "help meet" to help and work with him. Sin entered the world through Satan, who caused rebellion against God. Sin came through Adam and Eve's fall in the Garden of Eden. Man thought then, and still thinks now, that he does not need God. However, man does not know that his life, and everybody else's life, belongs to God. *"Wherefore, as by one man sin entered into the world, and death by sin; and so death passed upon all men, for that all have sinned."* **Romans 5:12**

WHAT IS SIN?

For all that is in the world, the lust of the flesh, and the lust of the eyes, and the pride of life, is not of the Father, but is of the world. **1 John 2:16** *"...and sin when it is full-grown, brings forth death."* **James 1:15** *"For the wages of sin is death..."* **Romans 6:23** But with Christ in a child's life, he will learn to deal with life's problems. He will know God is always there for him.

When you see your baby for the first time, you are filled with joy, knowing you brought forth this new life—with God's help. Some women do not feel this way—but that's another story. The shine and glow on a mother's face shows how much she loves her child. To hear his first cry and to hold him for the first time is something beautiful. Before a baby's first breath, he is in the darkness. When the baby is born, its surroundings are cold and noisy. He is insecure in a room filled with light. Yet the baby is still surrounded with love and comfort as he is held by those who love him. He hears the soothing voices of his parents, which surrounds him. That is the assurance that mothers are to give their newborns.

He is surrounded by love from the time the doctors who deliver him and his mouth and nose are suctioned to clear his airway to prevent choking; all so your baby can take his first breath. Even blankets are warmed to wrap his chilled body. All this is from the love of God's people. A team working together on the baby's behalf. Yes, it takes a village to care for a child! Yes, Baby, you are loved!

BONDING

Wrapped in a warm blanket, Baby is placed on his mother's chest. She holds the baby tenderly with tears of joy. Hopefully, Dad is close by. Now what? Will Baby be going home to a house of joy? I am by no means a doctor, psychologist, or social worker. But I know a child needs someone to take time to teach good righteous things to him. When Baby goes home with his parents, the nurturing should continue. *"Jesus to the children in his arms, put his hands upon them, and blessed them."* **Mark 10:16** So, now. Do it right! Love your baby!

I talk to a lot of young people. When I tell them about the goodness of God, they ask, "Can you tell me about Him?" Some of them have heard of Him. Some have spent time alone with Him in their despair and pain.

When I was a child, neighbors would watch out for and encourage me to do the right things—and to stay in school. The Village, to me, is thy neighbor. *"Thou shalt love thy neighbor as thyself."* **Matthew 19:19** Our neighbor is a person to love. God will give you the spirit of discernment to know who to trust. It is never right to hate anyone, even if we can justify it. Our neighbor can be anyone of any race, creed, or social background who is in need. In giving love, we can meet their needs. Neighbors can feed, clothe and give Godly love to your child. Wherever you live, there are needy people close by.

If there is a child in need, would you refuse to help, knowing you have the means to give? For instance, suppose a neighbor's children are grown and she kept boxes of their out-grown clothes and shoes in her attic. As a Villager, if she can see your children are in need of shoes and clothing, why not share what she has and make those children, in need, happy? That's a village! People who make up the village look out for one another.

TODDLER

As a toddler, you are guided in walking and talking. You are taught by your parents not to put harmful things in your mouth. Or not to put your finger in the electric wall socket or to touch fire. You are taught all things out of love for you. Oh, the joy when you first begin to walk, talk, and recognize family members! All this learning comes from God to you, along with the teachings of the parents, God has given you.

Parents, read to your child until he/she can read on their own. Continue sustained reading periods with your child. They will model your behavior.

Pre-school/Teen

A child starting school asks questions of parents and/or teachers. They seek God for answers. I've heard people say, "What you don't know can't hurt you." Do not believe that. It can. It is best to know the truth and it will set you free. Start paying attention in school. Behave and study hard to achieve to be successful. Ask your parents to take you to Sunday school and learn to grow in the ways of the Lord. Later, it will be beneficial to you.

Parents, Let the child know it is okay to cry. *"The tears of the oppressed, but they have no comforter—on the side of their oppressors there is power." **Ecclesiastes 4:1*** Also, make the child aware of incest or people touching their bodies inappropriately. Teach them to tell parents, teachers, family members, or someone whom they can trust in situations such as that. They should be taught that kind of behavior is not of God. *"None of you shall approach anyone who is near of kin to him, to uncover their nakedness." **Leviticus 18:6*** Never lieth with sister, or with beast, or father's wife (**Leviticus 20:11, Deuteronomy 28:20-23**).

Children learn what they see and are taught. In order for children to grow to love and trust, their homes should be loving and peaceful. Teach him that he will have friends throughout life, just from being friendly. *"A man who has friends, must shew himself friendly."* **Proverbs 18:24** When fussing and fighting occur in front of children, they learn to fuss and fight. Set a good example for your child. If they are in the will of God, they can tell others who are doing wrong about His goodness. However, if the ones the child is trying to reach continue to do wrong, the child will know that their company is bad for them and will choose to isolate themselves from the wrong doers.

Teach your child to clean and pick up behind himself. When he sees you cleaning, he too will clean. He will grow to be responsible and learn how to keep things in order. Reward your child when he does good things; such as making good grades in school. God rewards us when we follow His word.

"Chasten thy son while there is hope, and let not thy soul spare for his crying. A man of great wrath shall suffer punishment." **Proverbs 19:18,19** *"Withhold not correction from the child; for if thou punish him, he shall not die. Thou shall deliver his soul from hell."* **Proverbs 23:13,14** *"There are many devices in a man's heart; nevertheless the counsel of the Lord, that shall stand. He shall not be visited with evil"* **Proverbs 19:21,23** Some parents fear they will detach their relationship with their child. But correction will not kill children and it may prevent them from foolish moves that will. Teach your child the Ten Commandments. Instruct him to put them in his heart and to study them. *"The wise in heart will receive*

commandments." ***Proverbs 10:8*** Be a parent and not a friend. It is important to be involved in the child's life in all aspects. Instill a sense of short and long term goals in your child's life.

YOUNG ADULT

In this day and age, young adults search for purpose. They want to make fast money; often in the wrong way. Fights break out among their peers for territory or turf. But little do they know they have no claims to it. Did they buy the land they stand on? It is theirs? Even the drugs they sell are not theirs. Money will come. Because God has a plan for your life through tithes and offerings—and *work*. But first get a good education and learn. There are so many opportunities out there. So many leaders who came before you, died for these causes. Learn about these leaders and put your best foot forward! Do not waste your mind on foolishness. Be the proper young adult God wants you to be. Pull up your pants! Present yourself Holy. Try not to fight. *"A soft answer turneth away wrath; but grievous words stir up anger."* **Proverbs 15:1**

Parents, teach the scriptures to the child early. This will prepare him to be a strong person if he sees and hears sadness in his home. Teach him to appreciate his home. Help him understand there are so many homeless children who wish they could have a clean bed to lie in or a good meal to fill their empty stomachs. He should be reminded that the food he eats is purchased from hard work; and in some cases, given from free services. Teach him to be thankful for clothes and shoe on his feet. And to be especially thankful to God for family and friends who are willing to take him in, should the need arise. *"In every way give thanks; for this is the will of God in Christ Jesus concerning you." 1 Thessalonians 5:8.*

By now, you, as a young adult, should have learned to be God fearing. You now know that you can depend on God to help when you are in need, knowing His grace and mercy abounds. You should obey your parents, as God leads you. As your faith grows in them, you will prevent them from heartaches. And when you obey God, you too will be blessed.

When addressing an adult, you should say, "Yes, mam. No, mam. Yes, sir. No, sir." What has happened to politeness in some children? We must train our children to be polite to others. Manners go a long way. One day, I took my grand-daughter to a clothing store to purchase a sweater. The saleslady asked her if her sweater fit. She replied, "Yes, mam." The saleslady was shocked to hear the politeness in my grand-daughter. Some children today were never taught manners like this and have no respect for adults. *"Even a child is known by its deeds." **Proverbs 20:11***

Honor your mother and father (**Proverbs 1:8, Exodus 20:12**). If a child does not listen to his parents, destruction will follow (**Proverbs 15:5, 10:11, 28:7, 20:20, 22:15, Colossians 3:20, Luke 2:51, Ephesians 6, Deuteronomy 6**). When a child obeys his parents, there will be peace in their souls. They will be delighted in the child (**Proverbs**

29:17). You must honor your parents for long life upon the earth (**Ephesians 6, Exodus 20**).

If you do not understand the Bible, ask God to help you retain and comprehend what you are reading. Ask Him to give you revelation knowledge to understand what the Holy Bible is telling you. Hearing and reading about the men of faith in the Bible will help build your faith in God. When we, as adults, do not listen to God, he chastens us. *"For whomever the Lord loveth, He chasteneth."* **Hebrews 12:6** You will learn to be a wise old man/woman as you grow in grace, wisdom and love. All this will reflect the nurturing you have received from your upbringing. All will tell your parents they are blessed in the Lord (**Proverbs 31**).

Parents, be good examples to your children so they can follow the same good path. Not the path to destruction, but to great success. Here are some examples:

> **Some fathers are in jail. Some children, by following their fathers' lifestyles, they too, end up incarcerated.**

> **Some parents work hard to obtain a high school diploma or college degree. Their children do the same.**

> **Some parents work hard and show that hard work brings money to buy food and other items needed to live. The children, in turn, also work. By following their**

parent's example, they learn if they don't work, they don't eat.

The bible also teaches us about tithing, which will bring on prosperity. *"Bring ye all the tithes into the storehouse that there may be meat in mine house, and prove me now herewith, saith the Lord of host, if I will not open unto you the windows of heaven, and pour you out a blessing that there shall not be room enough to receive it."* **Malachi 3:10.**

I am trying to tell you to live a good and long, prosperous life in the Lord. I am not saying trouble, trials, and tribulations will not come, because they will. But when the word of God is planted deep inside of you, it will cause you to stand firm in any situation. No matter what happens, you will survive.

Learn about Jesus Christ and his mother, Mary—a godly woman who lived a holy life. As you grow in Christ, your parents will see the God in you, and gladly, let God use you for His glory. Your mother will be like Mary, who did not fuss when her son Jesus, had work to do for God. She saw this early in his life and did not deny him of serving God.

They both wanted to serve and follow God with all their hearts, minds, souls, and strength. They surrendered to God because they knew deep in their hearts, it was the right thing to do. God will not force His love on anyone. And it was their wills to serve Him. They worshipped God with a humble spirit. They knew He would use them to teach others about His goodness. About His ways, His love, His laws, and the way they should go.

God's word is life (**John 1:1**). *"The blood of Jesus Christ cleanseth us from all sin."* **1 John 1:7** God sent his Holy Spirit to dwell with and show you good things and keep you from danger, if you abide in Him. *"Believe not every spirit, but try the spirits whether they are of God; because many false prophets are gone out into the world."* **1 John 4:1** Also read: **Matthew 26:41, Romans 8:14-16, 1 Corinthians 2:10, 3:16, 6:11 and 17, 12:3, Ephesians 5:9, 6:18, James 4:5**. Also, read scriptures on repentance and faith.

God will in no way cast you out. Try Him now! Can you feel the love he radiates around you? God gives us His life, totally.

Parents, please allow us to instill God in our children to cast out the crime rate that is covering our world today. Do not get me wrong. There are parents who teach children about God. However, some the children today, push God aside or put Him on hold until they need Him. They know He is not far from them. They know He is just call, a whisper, or a thought away. Some children have to learn the hard way before they realize God is real. Mothers, we must put all our trust in God. Stand, and wait for His salvation. He is not short of His promises to us.

As a young adult, college should be on your mind. All parents were not fortunate to go to college or even get a decent education. Maybe they could not afford it. However, look for avenues to find resources to go to college or a vocational school. Today, doors are open everywhere for those who desire a higher level of education. Be strong in the Lord and trust in Him to see you through.

Today's world is seemingly turned upside down. Teens are killing each other just to say they took a life; something they did not give. It is no longer races against races. It is about power. I learned a long time ago if you don't get a good education to obtain a better job or work for your money, you cannot and will not appreciate it. Most of all, without money, you don't eat.

My daughter was taught if you want a better life, put God first. Everything else will be added and given to you by God's grace and mercy. If He sees you take the first step, He will do the rest.

I went to vocational school and college for a better job. I wanted to have a decent life and more money. Welfare just wasn't cutting it for me. Waiting on one check and food stamps every month didn't last and it wasn't enough. My child saw me struggling in school and the sacrifices I made. She decided to do the same and finished college with two degrees.

Coming out of college without any experience, it can be hard to find the job you want sometimes. But we know that God will open doors for us. Some children think their parents owe them something. But hard work and trusting in God will take you a long way.

Parents, do not provoke your child. And mothers, be kind to your babies (**Ephesians 6:4**). Your child will see you as a blessing to him. Instill in your child the Goodness of God in thine heart, and with all thy soul, and with all thy might and these words shall be in thine heart and in your child's heart

(**Deuteronomy 6**). *"And ye shall teach them, your children, speaking of them when thou sittest in thine house, and when thou walkest by the way, when thou liest down, and when thou riseth up."* **Deuteronomy 11:19**

A loving home brings thoughtfulness, an eagerness to please, and kindness. This is where God abides. When the child knows the word of God, he will become wise with faith and learn the salvation of Jesus Christ. Even in all our faults and sins, God still loves us so! Oh, what a wonderful God we serve! His great love surrounds us always; even unto the ends of the earth!

I believe even when children are born with defects, it is not of God. He does not make mistakes. Our God is perfect in every way. In every situation, God has a plan for our lives. He will allow you to reach someone else in the same situation to show what the devil meant for bad, God made it good. Remember, God looks at the heart—not the body nor its infirmities. Remember, Jesus was not one that we could look upon and lust after. He had a pure heart.

Children are a blessing from God. In reading the Bible you will understand how much you mean to Him. *"Thus saith the Lord that made thee, and formed thee from the womb, which will help thee."* **Isaiah 44:2** *"Lo, children are a heritage from the Lord. And the fruit of the womb is His reward. As arrows are in the hand of a mighty man; so are children of the youth."* **Psalm 127:3,4** *"But thou art he that took me out of the womb."* **Psalm 22:9** *"Thou has covered me in my mother's womb."* **Psalm 139:13** *"Unless the Lord builds the house, its builders labor in vain."* **Psalm 127:1** *"Honor thy father and* *thy mother; that thy days may be long upon the land which the Lord thy God giveth thee." **Exodus 20:12***

*"Blessed is she who believed that what the Lord has said to her will be accomplished." **Luke 1:45***

"BE BLESSED"

Other Scriptures:

"Salvation cometh from God." Psalm 62:1

"The Lord is the strength of my life." Psalm 27:1

"For the wages of sin is death, but the gift of God is eternal life in Christ Jesus our Lord." Romans 6:23

Be saved: *"That if you confess with your mouth, Jesus is Lord, and believe in your heart that God raised Him from the dead, you will be saved."* Romans 10:9,10

Repent: *"And the times of this ignorance God winked at; but now commandeth all men every where to repent."* Acts 17:30

"Grace is a gift from God." Ephesians 2:8

REFLECTION PAGES

Reflection Pages

REFLECTION PAGES

REFLECTION PAGES

_____

_____

_____

_____

_____

_____

_____

_____

_____

_____

_____

_____

_____

_____

_____

_____

_____

REFLECTION PAGES

REFLECTION PAGES

REFLECTION PAGES

_____

_____

_____

_____

_____

_____

_____

_____

_____

_____

_____

_____

_____

_____

_____

_____

_____

_____

Reflection Pages

REFLECTION PAGES

Reflection Pages

Reflection Pages

REFLECTION PAGES

_____

_____

_____

_____

_____

_____

_____

_____

_____

_____

_____

_____

_____

_____

_____

_____

_____

_____

REFLECTION PAGES

REFLECTION PAGES

_____

_____

_____

_____

_____

_____

_____

_____

_____

_____

_____

_____

_____

_____

_____

_____

_____

_____

Reflection Pages

REFLECTION PAGES

_____

_____

_____

_____

_____

_____

_____

_____

_____

_____

_____

_____

_____

_____

_____

_____

REFLECTION PAGES

REFLECTION PAGES

REFLECTION PAGES

Reflection Pages

Printed in the United States
By Bookmasters